Putting

the **One Minute Manager®**

to Work

Also by Ken Blanchard

Self Leadership and the One Minute Manager (with Susan Fowler and Laurence Hawkins), 2005

The Secret (with Mark Miller), 2004

Customer Mania! (with Jim Ballard and Fred Finch), 2004

The Leadership Pill (with Marc Muchnick), 2003

Full Steam Ahead! (with Jesse Stoner), 2003

The Servant Leader (with Phil Hodges), 2003

The One Minute Apology™ (with Margret McBride), 2003

Zap the Gaps! (with Dana Robinson and Jim Robinson), 2002

Whale Done!™ (with Thad Lacinak, Chuck Tompkins, and Jim Ballard), 2002

High Five! (with Sheldon Bowles), 2001

Management of Organizational Behavior: Utilizing Human Resources (with Paul Hersey), 8th edition, 2000

Big Bucks! (with Sheldon Bowles), 2000

Leadership by the Book (with Bill Hybels and Phil Hodges), 1999

The Heart of a Leader, 1999

Gung Ho!® (with Sheldon Bowles), 1998

Management by Values (with Michael O'Connor), 1997

Mission Possible (with Terry Waghorn), 1996

Empowerment Takes More Than a Minute (with John P. Carlos and Alan Randolph), 1996

Everyone's a Coach (with Don Shula), 1995

We Are the Beloved, 1994

Raving Fans® (with Sheldon Bowles), 1993

Playing the Great Game of Golf, 1992

The One Minute Manager Builds High Performing Teams (with Don Carew and Eunice Parisi-Carew), 1989

The One Minute Manager Meets the Monkey (with William Oncken, Jr., and Hal Burrows), 1989

The Power of Ethical Management (with Norman Vincent Peale), 1988

The One Minute Manager Gets Fit (with D.W. Edington and Marjorie Blanchard), 1986

Leadership and the One Minute Manager (with Patricia Zigarmi and Drea Zigarmi), 1985

Organizational Change Through Effective Leadership (with Robert H. Guest and Paul Hersey), 2nd edition, 1985

The One Minute Manager® (with Spencer Johnson), 1982

The Family Game: A Situational Approach to Effective Parenting (with Paul Hersey), 1979

Putting

the One Minute Manager®

to Work

Ken Blanchard
Robert Lorber, Ph.D.

wm

WILLIAM MORROW
An Imprint of HarperCollinsPublishers

 *The Symbol*

The One Minute Manager's symbol—a one-minute readout from the face of a modern digital watch—is intended to remind each of us to take a minute out of our day, every now and then, to look into the faces of the people we manage. And to realize that *they* are our most important resources.

 *Introduction*

In the last episode of *The One Minute Manager*, the bright young man who was searching for an effective manager learned the One Minute Manager's three secrets. He immediately realized that they were the key to effective management.

The young man learned his lessons well. Eventually he became a One Minute Manager.

He set One Minute goals.

He gave One Minute Praisings.

He delivered One Minute Reprimands.

In this second episode of *The One Minute Manager*, a veteran manager wonders whether using the three secrets on a day-to-day basis will really make a difference where it counts—in performance. He seeks the answer from a new One Minute Manager. In the process he learns how to put One Minute Management to work in a systematic way to achieve excellence.

This book is meant to be a companion to the original book. It is a practical tool that can be used independently to implement the three secrets but will probably be a richer experience if you have first read *The One Minute Manager*.

We hope you apply and use what the veteran manager learns and it makes a difference in your life and in the lives of those who work with you.

KENNETH BLANCHARD, PH.D.
ROBERT LORBER, PH.D.

Putting the One Minute Manager to Work

 *Foreword*

Today more than ever it's obvious that the gap between learning and doing is much bigger than the gap between ignorance and knowledge, particularly in the areas of leadership and management. As we say in *Putting the One Minute Manager to Work,* "Most companies spend all their time looking for the next new management concept and never follow up on what they just taught their people." Recently I got a call from a company that told me they had Steve Covey speak last year and they wanted me to speak this year. I said, "That's great. I'll call Tom Peters and see what he's doing next year."

Knowing the reality of the gap between learning and doing, I went to Bob Lorber about writing *Putting the One Minute Manager to Work.* Everybody loved *The One Minute Manager* and thought it was great, but I was fearful they wouldn't put the concepts into practice. For many years Bob was one of the top productivity improvement experts in the country. He built his own consulting firm, Lorber Kamai, and helped companies of every size and shape keep their commitments and follow through on their good intentions.

That's what *Putting the One Minute Manager to Work* is all about. If you love *The One Minute Manager* and really want to use the three secrets of

One Minute Goal Setting, One Minute Praising, and One Minute Reprimands in your organization, you're going to find out exactly how to do that in this book. I've gotten so cocky about the concepts in *Putting the One Minute Manager to Work* that I have offered companies a five-to-one money-back guarantee.

What I mean by a five-to-one guarantee is this: If the company doesn't return to their bottom line five times the amount they pay us to implement the concepts in this book, we'll make up the difference. People say to me, "How did you get so cocky?" I say, "It's real easy. Nobody ever follows up on anything." How many diets does it take to lose weight? Only the one you stick to. *Putting the One Minute Manager to Work* is a book that has concepts you ought to stick to. If you believe in them and follow them, they'll make a difference in your organization and in your people.

One of the joys in writing this book was working with Bob Lorber, whom I've known for more than twenty-five years now. Not only is Bob an accomplished professional, he is a first-rate human being as well. I am proud to have worked with him on *Putting the One Minute Manager to Work*. We wrote this book together more than twenty years ago and are excited about reissuing this edition, which is probably more relevant now than it was then. So enjoy, apply, and use. If you don't, then give me a call so I can give you a One Minute Reprimand.

—KEN BLANCHARD

TO

Our wives, Margie and Sandy,
for their constant love
and support throughout
the highs and lows
of our lives

Contents

WHEN the veteran manager finished reading *The One Minute Manager*, he put the book down on his coffee table. He leaned back with a questioning look. He had first read the book at the office but had brought it home to give it another reading.

"Even after a second time through," he thought to himself, "I cannot argue with the logic of the three secrets of the One Minute Manager. But if I practice them, will I actually become a more productive manager?"

The veteran manager decided to do something about his question. The next morning he would call a manager in a town a few hours away who had, in recent years, turned a troublesome company into a very profitable enterprise. The veteran had read a newspaper interview with this manager in which he had credited much of his success to practicing One Minute Management. In fact, he now called himself a "One Minute Manager."

THE next morning when the veteran manager got to his office, he called the new One Minute Manager. He introduced himself and asked the manager if he could see him sometime that week and talk about One Minute Management. The veteran had been warned what the answer might be but he was still surprised when the One Minute Manager actually said, "Come anytime except Wednesday morning. That's when I meet with my key people. To be honest with you, I don't have much else scheduled this week. You pick the time."

"I'll be over tomorrow morning at ten," said the veteran manager, chuckling to himself. When he hung up the phone he thought, "This ought to be interesting. I'm sure I'll get my questions answered."

When the veteran manager arrived at the One Minute Manager's office, the secretary said, "He's expecting you. Go right in."

As he entered the room, he found a man in his late forties standing by the window looking out.

The veteran manager coughed and the One Minute Manager looked up. He smiled and said, "Good to see you. Let's sit down over here." He led the manager to a conversation area in the corner of the room.

"Well, what can I do for you?" the One Minute Manager asked as he sat down.

"I have read *The One Minute Manager* and so have my people," the veteran manager began. "I'm enthusiastic right now and so are they, but that has happened before when a new management system has been introduced. My question is how do you put One Minute Management to work in a way that turns the secrets into usable skills and makes a difference where it really counts—in performance?"

"Before I attempt to answer that question," said the One Minute Manager, "let me ask you one. What do you think the message of One Minute Management is?"

"It's quite simple," said the veteran manager. "If you have a sheet of paper I'll write it down for you."

The One Minute Manager went over to his desk and got a pad. He gave it to the veteran manager. Without pausing the veteran manager wrote:

*

People Who Produce
Good Results

Feel Good
About Themselves

*

"That's an interesting twist," said the One Minute Manager, gesturing to a plaque on the wall behind his desk. It read: PEOPLE WHO FEEL GOOD ABOUT THEMSELVES PRODUCE GOOD RESULTS. "Why did you change it?"

"I think it better represents the essence of One Minute Management," insisted the veteran manager, "and besides, it's more consistent with what you teach."

"Consistent?" questioned the One Minute Manager.

"Yes," responded the veteran manager firmly. "You say that one of the key ingredients to a One Minute Praising is to be specific—to tell the person exactly what he or she did right."

"That's true," said the One Minute Manager.

"Then praisings, which help make people feel good about themselves, are not effective unless those people have done something positive first," smiled the veteran manager, feeling he had the One Minute Manager trapped.

"**Y**OU'RE a tough man," laughed the One Minute Manager, "and you really have a handle on One Minute Management. I think I can learn a few things from you. I'll feel good about sharing as much as I can too."

"I doubt if you will learn much from me," said the veteran manager. "I'm just a 'street fighter' who has survived."

"Can't take a compliment, huh?" mused the One Minute Manager. "Most people can't quite accept being praised."

"I would imagine that's because we've never gotten much practice receiving praisings," said the veteran manager. "And it's not easy to do something that you're not used to doing, even if you believe in it."

"Right," said the One Minute Manager. "One of the reasons it's hard to implement One Minute Management is that people will have to change some of their old behavior. And focusing on and changing how people treat each other in organizations is something that gets only lip service. Most top managers think that management training is just a fringe benefit—a nice little frill they can give all their employees every year. That's why I have that saying on the wall," he added as he gestured to a plaque on the other side of the room. It said:

*

*Most Companies
Spend All Their Time
Looking For Another
Management Concept*

*And
Very Little Time
Following Up The One
They Have Just Taught
Their Managers*

*

"That's so true," said the veteran manager. "And people do the same thing. They're always looking for the next quick fix rather than using what they have already learned. They go from one diet program to another diet program, one exercise plan to another, without following the last program."

"Then they wonder why they don't lose weight or build up their hearts," said the One Minute Manager. "It reminds me of a story of the man who slipped and fell off a cliff while hiking on a mountaintop. Luckily he was able to grab a branch on his way down. Holding on for dear life, he looked down only to see a rock valley some fifteen hundred feet below. When he looked up it was twenty feet to the cliff where he had fallen.

"Panicked, he yelled, 'Help! Help! Is anybody up there? Help!'

"A booming voice spoke up. 'I am here and I will save you if you believe in me.'

"'I believe! I believe!' yelled back the man.

"'If you believe me,' said the voice, 'let go of the branch and then I will save you.'

"The young man, hearing what the voice said, looked down again. Seeing the rock valley below, he quickly looked back up and shouted, 'Is there anybody else up there?'"

"That's a good one," laughed the veteran manager. "That's exactly what I don't want to do—hold on to the branch and keep looking for another system. One Minute Management is the way I want to manage and be managed. All I want to know is how to put it to work so that it lasts and makes a difference."

"Then you came to the right place," said the One Minute Manager. "What problems have you been having using the three secrets?"

"I think the main difficulty I have had," said the veteran manager, "has been turning the secrets into skills. That is, knowing when to do what. For example, I think that sometimes I'm reprimanding when I should be goal setting and at other times I'm goal setting when I should be reprimanding."

"I had the same trouble," said the One Minute Manager, "until I learned my ABC's."

"I know you're not talking about the ABC's of school days," said the veteran. "So what do you mean?"

"**N**O, I'm not referring to the alphabet, but the ABC's are a way of getting back to basics. They've helped this organization make the transition from secrets to skills. We knew the three secrets of One Minute Management, and we were really enthusiastic, but they weren't influencing performance significantly until we learned the ABC's of management," said the One Minute Manager. Turning to the blackboard on his office wall he wrote:

```
A = Activators
B = Behavior
C = Consequences
```

Then he began his explanation:

"*A* stands for *activators*. Activators are those things that have to be done by a manager before someone can be expected to accomplish a goal. *B* stands for *behavior* or performance. It is what a person says or does. *C* stands for *consequences* or what a manager does after someone accomplishes or attempts to accomplish a goal. If managers can learn to understand and deliver the necessary activators (A) and consequences (C), they can ensure more productive behavior (B) or performance."

"So learning your ABC's is a good key to good performance," said the veteran.

"It certainly is," said the One Minute Manager. "A number of companies have realized that they can experience significant performance improvement by following up and getting their managers to actually use the ABC's and other implementation strategies I'll teach you."

"Could you tell me more about them?" said the veteran manager.

"I think what's interesting about these companies," said the One Minute Manager, "is that they are from a variety of businesses and industries, but in every case real bottom-line improvements were experienced. They worked on such things as productivity (both quality and quantity), safety, retention, sales, costs, and profits."

"You've got my interest," said the veteran manager. "I think I'd better learn more about the ABC's if I want to put One Minute Management to work and make those kinds of differences."

"Why don't you go see one of our people, Tom Connelly," said the One Minute Manager. "He increased retention and made major performance improvements in one of our departments. He can tell you all about the ABC's."

"I'd love to meet him," said the veteran manager. "But before you call him, let me ask you one more thing. Do you always talk in threes? First three secrets and now ABC's."

"Not always," smiled the One Minute Manager. "But I believe in the KISS method: Keep It Short and Simple. I don't think people can remember a whole lot of things, particularly if they are going to use what they have learned."

"Isn't KISS usually Keep It Simple, Stupid?" wondered the veteran manager.

"Yes," admitted the One Minute Manager. "But since One Minute Management is a positive approach to managing people, we use a positive way to express the concept."

"I knew you'd have a good explanation," smiled the veteran. "I'm looking forward to meeting Connelly."

The One Minute Manager dialed a number and said, "Tom, I have an experienced manager here who wants to learn his ABC's. Are you free?"

Although the veteran could not hear everything clearly, he smiled as he thought he heard Connelly say, "Send him over. I've just gotten back. I was out having fun catching my people doing things right."

"Stop back when you are finished talking with Tom," said the One Minute Manager as he led the veteran manager to the door.

"Sure will!" said the veteran manager. "Thanks for your time."

W

HEN the veteran manager got to Connelly's office, he found a sharply dressed man in his mid-forties.

As Connelly got up from his desk and introduced himself, the veteran manager got right to the point: "Your boss told me you could give me the real lowdown on the ABC's of management."

"I'll try," said Connelly. "Let me start off by giving you this summary that we use so everyone can remember the ABC's." He handed the veteran manager a chart.

The ABC's of Management: A Summary

The term:

A	B	C
ACTIVATOR	**BEHAVIOR**	**CONSEQUENCE**

What it means:

What a manager does **before** performance	Performance: What someone says or does	What a manager does **after** performance

Examples:

One Minute Goal Setting • Areas of Accountability • Performance standards • Instructions	• Writes report • Sells product • Comes to work on time • Misses deadline • Types letter • Makes mistake • Fills order	***One Minute Praising*** • Immediate, specific • Shares feelings ***One Minute Reprimand*** • Immediate, specific • Shares feelings • Supports individual ***No Response***

The veteran manager read the chart very carefully. When he finished reading he looked up, smiled, and said, "So One Minute Goal Setting is an activator?"

"Yes," said Connelly. "An activator is like an ante in poker. It gets things started."

"If goal setting is an activator," said the veteran, "then you're not in the management game unless your people are clear on their key areas of responsibility (accountability) and what good performance in each of those areas looks like (performance standards)."

"That's why goal setting is the most important activator for managers to remember," said Connelly. "It starts the whole management process."

"Sounds good," affirmed the veteran manager. "Once people are activated, then they are ready to perform."

"They certainly are," said Connelly. "It's that performance that managers need to watch. Once you have asked someone to do something, what they say or do while trying to accomplish the desired task is their performance or behavior— the *B* of ABC's."

"Is what people think or feel considered behavior?" asked the veteran manager.

"No," said Connelly. "While thoughts and feelings are important, since they often determine what people do, they are not considered behavior because they are behind the eyeballs."

"In other words," jumped in the veteran, "you cannot see them."

"Right," said Connelly. "Once you get into thoughts and feelings, there's lots of room for complications and misunderstanding. If we stick to behavior, things are clearer because behavior can be observed and measured. As you can see from the chart, writing a report, selling a product, coming to work on time, missing a deadline, typing a letter, making a mistake, and filling an order are all behaviors."

"From that list, it seems that behavior can be either desirable or undesirable," commented the veteran manager.

"Right," said Connelly. "And how easily you are able to distinguish between the two depends on the goal-setting process. You see, if One Minute Goal Setting is done properly, the desired performance is stated in behavioral terms—that is, it can be seen (observed) and counted (measured). That is important because when you observe someone's behavior you want to be able to determine whether it is contributing toward the accomplishment of the goal (they are doing things right), or taking away from goal achievement (they are doing things wrong). That gives you an idea of how to respond as that person's boss."

"Respond?" said the veteran manager.

"Responding has to do with consequences," said Connelly. "The *C* in our ABC's. They are the responses managers give to people when they either perform a task or attempt to perform a task. Consequences follow or come after some performance."

"One Minute Praisings and One Minute Reprimands are obviously consequences," said the veteran manager.

"A One Minute Praising is an example of a positive consequence or response," said Connelly, "while a One Minute Reprimand is an example of a negative response. Whether positive or negative, the consequence has to be appropriate."

"Appropriate?" wondered the veteran manager.

"If you want people to stop doing something, give them a negative response like a One Minute Reprimand," said Connelly. "But if you want people to keep on doing something, or to improve or to learn something new, give them a positive consequence like a One Minute Praising."

"I find that using praisings and reprimands appropriately is not always easy," said the veteran manager.

"It certainly isn't," said Connelly. "One of the problems is that many managers seem to praise or reprimand their people depending on how they themselves feel on any given day, regardless of anyone's performance. If they are feeling good, they pat everyone on the back, and if they are in a bad mood, they yell at everyone."

"And I would imagine that if managers start doing that—that is, praising and reprimanding indiscriminately—their credibility will soon be shot," said the veteran manager.

"Good point," commented Connelly. "It reminds me of the story about the blind man who is walking down the street with his Seeing Eye dog. They get to a corner and while they are waiting for the light to change, the dog lifts his leg and urinates on the blind man's pants. When that happens, the blind man reaches into his pocket and takes out a dog treat. Then he bends down and looks as if he is about to give it to the dog. A bystander who has seen this whole thing can't contain himself any longer so he goes up to the blind man and says, 'Sir, it's probably none of my business but I noticed that your dog relieved himself on you and now you are about to give him a treat. Do you think that is really a good idea?' The blind man smiles and says, 'I'm not about to give my dog a treat. I just want to find out where his head is so I can kick him in the tail.'"

"That's beautiful," laughed the veteran. "When people see a manager isn't credible, that is confusing to them. If the blind man gave the dog a treat for inappropriate behavior like that and yelled at him when he really wasn't doing anything wrong, the dog would soon become confused and not know what to do. I have seen confusion like that in organizations. Therefore I'd better make sure I understand about consequences."

"Good idea," said Connelly.

"As I told the One Minute Manager," continued the veteran manager, "my problem is more confusion about when to be reprimanding and when to be goal setting than any difficulty between reprimanding and praising. Do you have any suggestions?"

"Yes," said Connelly. "Remember, you can effectively reprimand only winners because you can then end your negative feedback with a praising like: 'You're one of my best people—this recent performance is so unlike you.' You can't do that with people who are learning to perform and therefore have no past good performance history."

"So what do you do when people who are learning make a mistake?" queried the veteran.

"I would go back to goal setting and ante up again. You can summarize it this way," said Connelly, writing on his pad of paper:

When to Reset Goals

AND

When to Reprimand

If a person:
CAN'T DO something ———► Go Back to Goal Setting *(A Training Problem)*

If a person:
WON'T DO something ———► Reprimand *(An Attitude Problem)*

"That's very helpful," said the veteran. "So you never reprimand learners."

"No," said Connelly, "or you will immobilize them and make them even more insecure."

"So reprimands do not teach skills," observed the veteran manager. "They can just change attitudes—get skilled people back to using their abilities."

"Precisely," said Connelly. "After you reset goals with someone you are training, you don't leave that person alone. Observe the performance again and then either praise progress or go back to goal setting once more."

"It seems to me from what you're saying," commented the veteran, "that there are five steps to training a learner to be a good performer:

1. **Tell** (what to do)

2. **Show** (how to do)

Then

3. **Let** the person **try**

4. **Observe** performance

And

5. **Praise** progress
             or
       Redirect

"You're on the money," said Connelly. "That's a good summary of how to train someone."

"What if you keep redirecting some of your people again and again and they just don't show any progress?" questioned the veteran manager.

"You talk to such a person about career planning," laughed Connelly. "In other words, he or she just might not be in the right job."

"Given the importance of redirecting in training," said the veteran, "why don't you list it as a consequence on your ABC chart?"

"That's a good question," said Connelly. "I heard you were sharp. Redirecting certainly does follow behavior. But I never thought of it as a consequence. I'll have to add it."

"I do see from the chart, though," said the veteran, "that you have 'no response' listed as a consequence."

"It's the most popular with American managers," said Connelly. "So often managers simply ignore their people's performance, and it doesn't work."

"What do you mean?" said the veteran manager.

"What happens if you get no response after performing a task?" asked Connelly. "Your manager doesn't do or say anything."

"In the beginning, I'd try harder," said the veteran. "I'd think, 'If only I try harder maybe my boss will notice.'"

"What if your boss still doesn't notice or respond?" asked Connelly.

"After a while, I'd start doing it 'half-fast,'" smiled the veteran, getting into the humor that the One Minute Manager and his people seemed to enjoy. "Since no one seems to care whether I do this or not, why kill myself?"

"Unless you were doing something that was motivating to you in and of itself," said Connelly.

"If that occurred you would be confused about the difference between work and play," said the veteran manager.

"That's an interesting way to put it," said Connelly. "If you are doing what you enjoy at work, you will continue to do it well regardless of whether anyone notices and pats you on the back. But generally, no response to good performance, like a negative consequence, tends to decrease the possibility of that performance being repeated."

"Let me see if I have all this straight," said the veteran manager as he showed Connelly his notes:

*

*Only
Positive
Consequences*

*Encourage
Good
Future
Performance*

*

"That's the headline," said Connelly, "and yet, what are the most frequent responses managers give to the performance of their people?"

"Negative or no response at all," said the veteran manager. "As we both know, the American way of managing seems to be: When people perform well, their managers do nothing. When they make a mistake, their managers 'hit' them."

"It's the old 'leave alone-zap' technique," said Connelly with a smile. "Not a very effective way of motivating people."

"But a very easy habit to fall into," said the veteran manager. "I've done it myself. I can see now that if I'm going to manage my people, I'd better learn to manage consequences."

"That's an important lesson to learn," said Connelly. "Most people think that activators have a greater influence on performance than consequences. And yet, only fifteen to twenty-five percent of what influences performance comes from activators like goal setting, while seventy-five to eighty-five percent of it comes from consequences like praisings and reprimands."

"You're saying that what happens after a person does something has more impact than what happens before?" questioned the veteran skeptically.

"That's it," said Connelly. "Performance is determined mainly by consequences. That's why the One Minute Manager is so vehement about the importance of follow-up. We believe you should spend ten times as much time following up your management training as it took to plan and conduct an initial program. Otherwise people will revert back to old behavior within a short period."

"Yes, but if you don't set goals, the chances are low that people will do what you want them to do in the first place," interjected the veteran manager.

"Right," said Connelly. "But all the goal setting in the world without any managing of consequences—praising good performance and reprimanding poor—will only get things started and provide short-term success for a manager. In other words, managers will get the performance they want only when they are there, but when they are not there, people may or may not engage in the behavior the manager wants. We have a saying that emphasizes the importance of managing consequences," said Connelly as he pointed to a plaque on the wall.

*

*As A Manager
The Important Thing
Is Not What Happens
When You Are There*

*But
What Happens When
You Are Not There*

*

"That's so true," said the veteran. "I can always get the performance I want from people, even from my kids at home, when I am there. But I'm not around all the time. In fact, I think I spend as much, if not more, time at work with my peers (at the same level in the organization) and with my boss as I do with my subordinates."

"So the way you can really tell how good a manager you are," said Connelly, "is not by what happens when you are there, but by what happens when you're not there. And the secret to getting good performance from your people when you're *not* there is how effectively you deliver consequences when you *are* there—both praisings and reprimands."

"It is clear to me now," said the veteran manager, "what you meant when you said activators are important for starting good performance—getting it done the first time—but what really determines and influences whether that desired performance will be repeated when you are not there is what happens after the original performance. The 'leave alone-zap' approach just frustrates and alienates people."

"The whole purpose of teaching our people their ABC's," said Connelly, "is to ensure that they sequence One Minute Goal Setting, One Minute Praisings, and One Minute Reprimands in the proper order. It's a behavioral reminder."

"You have certainly shown me how to begin to turn the secrets into skills," said the veteran. "I don't think I'll ever forget when to do what anymore. But let me ask one more question. You have been emphasizing the importance of clear, good goal setting, followed by One Minute Praisings for good performance. I seem to have lost the idea of the effective use of One Minute Reprimands. Could you share with me some of the positive uses of reprimands again?"

"You might want to talk to the One Minute Manager about the effective use of One Minute Reprimands," said Connelly. "He loves to teach that secret, and besides, he would be willing to answer any questions you have about One Minute Goal Setting and One Minute Praisings as well."

"That's a good idea," said the veteran manager. "I certainly have taken up enough of your time."

"That's OK," said Connelly. "I have enjoyed it. Besides, knowing my ABC's has really helped me free up a lot of my time."

"I hope it does the same for me," said the veteran.

A S the veteran manager left Connelly's office, he found his mind going a mile a minute. Connelly had been quite helpful. As he approached the One Minute Manager's office, the manager's secretary smiled. "Did you have a good meeting with Tom Connelly?" she asked.

"I sure did," the veteran manager replied, returning her smile. "Could I see the boss?"

"Go right in," she said. "He was wondering if you were coming back."

As the veteran entered the office, he found the One Minute Manager looking out his favorite window. He turned as he heard the veteran manager enter.

"You were with Connelly for quite a while. The two of you must have gotten along quite well," he said.

"It was most helpful," said the veteran. "But I have some concerns about the use of reprimands," he went on. "In teaching me the ABC's, Connelly seemed to stress the importance of praisings but downplayed the use of reprimands. I know you believe in delivering bad news sometimes. Maybe I just need some reorientation."

"The best way for me to respond to your concerns about reprimanding," replied the One Minute Manager, "is to start by talking about managing winners—people with proven track records. Winners are easy to supervise. All you have to do is ante up One Minute Goals and then they are off."

"That fits with my experience," said the veteran manager. "While everyone likes a pat on the back once in a while, you don't have to praise winners very much. They usually beat you to the punch. Besides not praising winners very much, you don't often have to reprimand them either, do you?"

"No!" said the One Minute Manager. "Good performers are usually self-correcting. If they make a mistake, they fix it before anyone else notices."

"But everyone makes a mistake sometimes that he or she is unaware of," stated the veteran manager.

"Then you may have to reprimand," said the One Minute Manager. "However, if they know the three secrets, good performers don't resent it because of the way you deliver that reprimand."

"I assume you are talking about ending the reprimand with a praising," commented the veteran manager.

"Precisely," said the One Minute Manager.

"Connelly cleared up for me why you don't reprimand a learner, but I still have trouble understanding why you praise someone at the end of a reprimand," said the veteran manager.

"Remember, you only reprimand when you know the person can do better," the One Minute Manager reminded him. "When you leave your people after a reprimand, you want them to be thinking about what they did wrong, not about the way you treated them."

"I don't understand," the veteran hesitated.

"**L**ET me see if I can explain it this way," said the One Minute Manager. "Most people not only don't end their reprimands with a praising, they give the person a parting shot: 'If you think you're going to get promoted, you have another think coming.' Now when you leave that person, especially if there is a co-worker within earshot, what do you think these folks will be talking about? How you treated the person you were reprimanding or what the person did wrong?"

"How you treated the person," said the veteran manager.

"Precisely," said the One Minute Manager. "They're talking about what an SOB you are. And yet that person did something wrong. If you end your reprimand with a praising, you will be telling the person, 'You are OK but your behavior isn't!' Then when you leave, the person will be thinking about what he or she did wrong. If for any reason he tries to badmouth you to co-workers, they will stop it by saying, 'What are you getting so excited about? He said you were one of his best people. He just doesn't want you to make that mistake again.'"

"I think I understand what you're saying about ending with a praising," said the veteran manager. "See if this is a good summary comment." He showed his notes to the One Minute Manager. They said:

*

*When You
End A Reprimand
With A Praising*

*People Think
About*
Their *Behavior*
Not
Your *Behavior*

*

"That's very well put," said the One Minute Manager. "I'm reminded of a personal experience I had that proves your point. One Friday night my wife said to me, 'Great manager of people . . .' Whenever she says that I know our kids have done something wrong and I am about to get the problem dumped in my lap. She had just caught Karen [our fifteen-year-old daughter] sneaking out of the house with a bottle of vodka on the way to the football game.

"'I think I will kill her,' said my wife. 'Could you take over?'

"I have a lot of respect for single parents because there is no one in the bullpen they can call on. We have always had a strategy: If one of us is out of control, we throw the ball to the other.

"Since I had just learned about the reprimand, I thought this might be a good opportunity to see if it worked. I said, 'Where is Karen?' My wife said, 'She's in the kitchen.' So I went right out to the kitchen and found Karen standing there looking like she was about to be sent to the dungeon. I walked right up to her and put my hand gently on her shoulder. I said, 'Karen, Mom tells me she just caught you sneaking out of the house with a bottle of vodka. Let me tell you how I feel about that. I can't believe it. How many times have I told you the way kids get killed is to have some kid drinking and driving. And to be sneaking around with a bottle of vodka . . .'

"Now I knew that the rule of the reprimand was that you only have about thirty seconds to share your feelings."

"I bet you wanted two hours," said the veteran.

"You better believe it," laughed the One Minute Manager. "Some parents take a whole weekend. Your child does something wrong on Friday night and you chew the kid out. A half hour later you see the same kid and you say, 'Let me tell you one other thing. . . .' Then you see the kid the next morning and you say, 'Let me tell you about your friends too. . . .' You spend the whole weekend making everyone miserable over one misbehavior.

"The rule about the reprimand is that you only have thirty seconds to share your feelings, and when it's over—it's over. Don't keep beating on the person for the same mistake.

"Recognizing all this, I had to come to a screeching halt in sharing my feelings with Karen. It was at this point that I realized the importance of pausing for a moment of silence in between sharing your feelings and the last part of the reprimand. It permits you to calm down and at the same time lets the person you are reprimanding feel the intensity of your feelings. So I took a deep breath while Karen was swallowing hard. Then I said, 'Let me tell you one other thing, Karen. I love you. You're a real responsible kid. Mom and I normally don't have to worry about you. This sounds like some other kid. You're better than that. That's why Mom and I are not going to let you get away with that kind of behavior.'

"Then I gave her a hug and said, 'Now get off to the game but remember, you're better than that.'"

"I'm not sure I would have let her go to the game after something like that," said the veteran. "I bet she couldn't believe it herself."

"She couldn't believe it," confirmed the One Minute Manager. "But I told her, 'Now you know how I feel about teenage drinking and sneaking around. I know you're not going to do that again, so have a good time.'

"In the past, before I knew about the One Minute Reprimand, not only would I not have ended her reprimand with a praising, I would have sent her to her room, screaming something like 'You're not going to another football game until you're twenty-five.'

"Now, if I had sent her to her room, what do you think she would have been thinking about? What she did wrong or how I had treated her?" asked the One Minute Manager.

"How you had treated her," said the veteran manager. "I bet she would have been on the phone immediately, telling her friends what a monster you were. Teenagers love to share parent stories."

"Absolutely," said the One Minute Manager. "And then she would have been psychologically off the hook for what she had done wrong, with all her attention focused on how I had treated her."

"What happened next?" asked the veteran, feeling he was in the middle of a soap opera.

"The next morning," continued the One Minute Manager, "when I was eating breakfast, Karen came downstairs. Wondering how I had done, I asked her, 'Karen, how did you like the way I dealt with the vodka incident last night?'

"'I hated it,' she said. 'You ruined the football game for me.'

"'I ruined the football game for you?'

"'Yes,' she said. 'Because all through the game I kept thinking about what I had done and how much I had disappointed you and Mom!'

"I smiled to myself and thought, 'It worked! It really worked! She was concentrating on what she had done wrong and not on how I had treated her.'"

"That was a very helpful, clear example," said the veteran manager. "I think I've got that part of the reprimand, but I'd like to ask you a couple more things about the One Minute Reprimand."

"Fire away," said the One Minute Manager. "Most of the questions we get about One Minute Management have to do with the reprimand."

"What if the person you are reprimanding—Karen, for example—starts to argue with you?" asked the veteran.

"You stop what you are saying right then," said the One Minute Manager, "and make it very clear to that person that this is not a discussion. 'I am sharing my feelings about what you did wrong, and if you want to discuss it later, I will. But for right now this is not a two-way discussion. I am telling you how I feel.'"

"That's helpful," said the veteran. "One other thing. If I buy praising someone at the end of a reprimand, why not begin a reprimand with a praising? When I did reprimands in the past, I used the 'sandwich approach': Pat 'em on the back, kick 'em in the butt, pat 'em on the back."

"I know that style well," said the One Minute Manager, "but I've learned that it is very important to keep praisings and reprimands separate. If you start a reprimand with a praising, then you will ruin the impact of your praising."

"Why?" asked the veteran manager.

"Because when you go to see a person just to praise him," said the One Minute Manager, "he will not hear your praising because he will be wondering when the other shoe will drop—what bad news will follow the good."

"So by keeping praisings and reprimands in order, you will let your people hear both more clearly," summarized the veteran. "What about more tangible punishments like demotion, being transferred, or some other penalty? Are they ever appropriate?"

"Our experience with the One Minute Reprimand," said the One Minute Manager, "suggests that you usually do not need to add some additional penalty. It is an uncomfortable enough experience."

"That was beautifully illustrated with Karen," said the veteran manager. "I think you really cleared up my questions about reprimands. And also, I can now see how learning the ABC's helps managers take their knowledge of One Minute Management and translate it into action. But how can you integrate One Minute Management into a total organizational program for performance improvement?"

"You have to pay the PRICE," said the One Minute Manager with a smile.

"What is PRICE?" asked the veteran manager.

"The PRICE system," said the One Minute Manager, "goes beyond the ABC's by providing managers with five easy-to-follow steps that can involve everyone in improving performance."

"It sounds fascinating," said the veteran, "but my head is already swimming from all that I have learned today."

"Why don't you stay overnight locally and we can get together at nine in the morning? I'll ask my secretary to make a reservation for you at the Osborn Hotel. The manager there is really excited about One Minute Management and has implemented a unique praising program designed to catch his employees doing things right. I think you will find it most interesting."

"Sounds good to me," said the veteran.

WHEN the veteran manager arrived at the hotel, he went straight to the registration desk. As he was checking in, the receptionist said, "Our customers are important to us. I wonder if I can ask you to do us a favor during your visit."

"Sure," said the veteran. "What is it?"

"We'd like you to take this book of 'praising coupons.'* If any of our employees treats you the way you like to be treated, would you tear off a coupon, write on the back what the employee did right, find out what his or her name is, and turn it in at the manager's office?"

"So all your customers are catching your employees doing things right," laughed the veteran. "I bet a praising comes with each coupon the manager receives."

"You read the Book," exclaimed the receptionist with a smile.

"I did. Your hotel really seems to be putting One Minute Management to work," said the veteran.

"It's a fantastic system!" responded the receptionist enthusiastically. "Have a nice evening."

---

*Drew Dimond, former district director of Holiday Inns, Inc., in Nashville, Tennessee, got excited about *The One Minute Manager* and decided to implement a praising-coupon program in one of his hotels. Gary Wood, the hotel manager, ran with the ball. The results described here are similar to those they have observed in this Holiday Inn.

After an early dinner, the veteran went straight to his room to relax. He was amazed by how well he had been treated by all the hotel employees. He had already given out three coupons—to the bellman, his waitress, and the maitre d'. Catching people doing things right was changing his whole attitude toward this hotel. The praising coupons made it his job as a guest not to complain but to compliment.

The next morning, the veteran manager packed his bags and headed downstairs. After having breakfast he checked out. On his way out of the hotel, he stopped by the manager's office to drop off his praising coupons. The manager happened to be there.

As he handed the manager his praising coupons, the veteran manager said, "I think this praising program of yours is a great idea. It's a very practical way to put One Minute Management to work. Have there been any tangible bottom-line effects of the program?"

"While we have only had the system in place for about five months," said the hotel manager, "we have already seen significant reductions in absenteeism and turnover. Our employees look forward to coming to work now because they are anxious to see if they can be caught doing something right. And we have not been giving any financial payoffs for coupons—just a pat on the back for a job well done."

"Do you think this program has changed the customers' attitudes, too?" wondered the veteran. "Absolutely!" said the hotel manager. "Our greatest improvement has been in guest inspection scores. Our guests are asked to rate the hotel on an ABCDF scale on such items as value/cost, appearance, service, and friendliness. Prior to the praising program fewer than seventy percent of the guests who filled out the guest inspections cards rated the hotel in the A to B range. After the first five months of the program, the scores are averaging over ninety percent A's and B's and we are getting three times as many returned cards."

"So your praising coupons are paying high dividends for you, your customers, and your employees," said the veteran manager.

"Yes," said the hotel manager. "Putting the One Minute Manager to work pays a good return on investment."

As the veteran manager shook hands with the hotel manager, he smiled and said, "My stay here has been very profitable to me too!"

WHEN the veteran arrived at the One Minute Manager's office, he found him in his usual pose by the window. When he sensed the veteran standing in the doorway, the One Minute Manager turned around and greeted him with a friendly handshake and offered the veteran a chair at the conference table.

"Well, did you enjoy your stay at the Osborn Hotel last night?" the One Minute Manager asked as he sat down.

"I certainly did," responded the veteran, "and you were right—it was unique!"

"I wanted you to experience," confided the One Minute Manager, "an attempt to put One Minute Management to work before we talked today. I thought it would help you understand our PRICE system better."

As the veteran manager was listening to the One Minute Manager, he noticed a new plaque on his desk. It read:

*

Don't Just Do Something—

Sit There

*

The veteran manager smiled because he knew how the usual frantic, yet inefficient, pace of most organizations demanded the opposite.

"My key people gave it to me," said the One Minute Manager, when he saw the veteran looking at the plaque. "They thought it symbolized the importance of goal setting as a means of avoiding the 'activity trap.'"

"The activity trap?" wondered the veteran manager.

"That's where people are running around trying to do things right before anyone has stopped to figure out the right things to do."

"Talking about doing things right," said the veteran, "What's the best way for me to learn PRICE?"

"Why don't you go and talk to Alice Smith," suggested the One Minute Manager. "She's one of our most creative managers. She helped us develop the PRICE system. Since she took over our sales operation, sales have skyrocketed."

As the One Minute Manager was calling Alice Smith, the veteran manager was smiling to himself. He thought, "They certainly have taken all the mystique out of managing people. I'll bet PRICE is really quite simple, but powerful."

"Well, Alice is all set to see you," said the One Minute Manager. "You can head over to her office right away. She is in the same building as Connelly but on the third floor."

WHEN the veteran manager got to Alice Smith's office, he found her working quietly at her desk. He thought to himself, "At last a One Minute Manager who seems to be doing some work."

She smiled as he entered. "So you want to know if the PRICE is right," she said as she beckoned the veteran to sit down.

"Corny but true," said the veteran. "I'm anxious to get started."

"That's important because the PRICE system is the nuts and bolts of how to put the One Minute Manager to work and make a difference every day in the performance and satisfaction of people on the job. But you have to listen carefully because now we take the three basic skills and turn them into five important steps."

Smith immediately went to the small blackboard behind her desk and wrote:

Pinpoint
Record
Involve
Coach
Evaluate

"**P**INPOINT is the process of defi
performance areas for people in observable,
measurable terms," began Smith. "In essence, it is
the performance areas that you would identify as
One Minute Goals."

"Suppose I told you I was concerned about my
work group," said the veteran manager, "and I
wanted to rekindle commitment from my people.
Would that be specific enough?"

"No," said Smith. "We can't improve morale,
poor attitude, laziness, or things like that without
more information."

"Isn't it important to deal with morale problems
in organizations?" asked the veteran manager.

"Sure it is, but I would have to pinpoint what
you mean by poor morale," explained Smith. "Do
you mean people are coming to work late, or
quality rejects are frequent, or people are
bickering at work? What do you mean by poor
morale?"

"So we need to stop managers from saying
things are good or bad," said the veteran, "and get
them to identify specifically what is happening."

"That's what pinpointing is all about," said
Smith, pleased by the veteran's ability to learn
quickly. "Establishing the areas you are going to
measure and how you are going to measure
them—for example, in quantity, quality, cost (on
or off budget), or timeliness."

"Where does that bring us?" interrupted the
veteran.

"**D**IRECT to RECORD," answered Smith. "Once you have pinpointed an area for improvement or a One Minute Goal, you want to be able to measure present performance and track progress in that area. You will notice I talk about areas that you want to improve, not problems. People have trouble admitting there are problems, but everyone has an area he or she would like to improve."

"You mean you would gather actual data on how often people are late to work, how frequently products are rejected because of quality, and the like?" asked the veteran.

"That's right," said Smith. "You want to take the guesswork out of performance improvement."

"What if someone says, 'You can't measure performance in my job!'" wondered the veteran manager.

"When a person tells us that," said Smith, "we suggest that maybe we should eliminate the position and see if we've lost anything. It's amazing how interested they suddenly get in establishing ways to identify goals and measure performance in their jobs."

"Could you give me an example," said the veteran, "of a performance-improvement area you ran through the PRICE system?"

"Yes," said Smith. "When I took over the department, the old sales manager told me, 'Phone contact needs improvement around here. Salespeople never make appointments with customers by phone. They think they have to be on the road all the time. When they get to the customer, he's often out for the morning, or he's busy and can't be interrupted. They have to wait to see him so they end up spending all their time in coffee shops. If they made appointments, they'd get twice as much done in half the time.'

"I asked, 'How do you know phone contact needs improvement?'

"'I just feel everything starts there,' he replied. 'That's always been an issue in this company.'

"Then I asked, 'Have you counted it? Is there any way to tell exactly the number of phone calls salespeople make to customers?'

"'Well,' he said, 'I could check their phone logs. Each salesperson is required to keep a daily log of calls right by his or her phone.'

"When I put a count to it, I found that making appointments was not a crucial issue for everyone. In fact, only three salespeople were delinquent in their phoning," Smith stated.

"By recording or measuring performance," said the veteran, "you attempt to make sure the need for improvement is real and not just a feeling. You don't want to 'fix what ain't broken.'"

"Precisely," said Smith. "It's most effective to plot the information on a graph," she explained as she pulled a folder from her desk file. "Here's an initial graph I made of appointment calls for one of my salespeople, Jack.

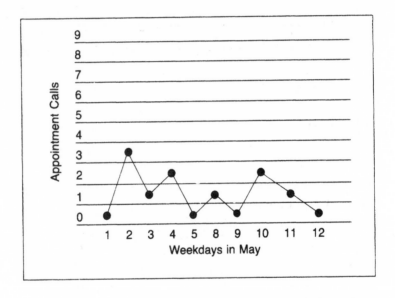

"On any of the graphs we use, we put time across the bottom or horizontal axis, and the pinpointed behavior along the side or the vertical axis," explained Smith. "The time element for Jack was weekdays in May for a two-week period and the behavior was the number of appointment calls made each day.

"**A**FTER I made the graph I calculated Jack's mean number of daily appointment calls. Over two weeks, he averaged one call a day. I knew improvement was needed since there was a difference between actual performance and what I thought was desired performance. I was ready for the INVOLVE step in PRICE."

"Is that when you informed Jack about his performance problem?" questioned the veteran. *Focus*

"Yes," said Smith. "Once you are aware *on* improvement is needed, you share that *total* information with whoever is responsible *improved* (accountable) for that area and/or can influence *across* performance in it—in our example it would be *the* Jack." *board*

"I bet when you've graphed all this performance *board* data on Jack and it shows clearly that he is not *and at* doing what you think he should be doing, there's a *all levels.* real temptation to let Jack have it," observed the veteran. "Give him the old 'leave alone-zap.'"

"There often is," said Smith, "but you need to control yourself. The time for reprimanding hasn't come yet. In fact, it is important to remember that graphs are not meant to be used as weapons, or as evidence in a managerial prosecution. They are designed to be used as training tools as well as nonjudgmental methods of feedback."

"So how do you share your graph with Jack?"

"Without judgment," said Smith. "And in a spirit of learning. You want Jack to learn, and you assume that Jack wants to improve. You know the saying around here:

*

*Feedback
Is The
Breakfast
Of
Champions*

Is there room in this system for high performers, not wanting to improve.

*

Would you base a promotion on absolute or relative achievement.

are we rewarding absolute achievements or relative achievements.

Resentment unequal treatment.

Payoff for improved performance.

"How true that is," affirmed the veteran. "But tell me, how do you involve someone like Jack besides giving him feedback on results?"

"You involve him in establishing the activators," said Smith. "That is, in deciding what has to be agreed upon before Jack can be expected to improve his performance to the desired level."

"Besides goal setting, what other agreements do you have to ante up?" smiled the veteran, enjoying the opportunity to show off what he had already learned.

"Coaching and evaluation strategies," answered Smith. "You need to agree about how you are going to supervise Jack as well as how he will be evaluated and what payoff he can anticipate for improved performance."

"Do you always involve your people in establishing One Minute Goals?" wondered the veteran manager.

"Yes, in most cases," said Smith. *"One Minute Management just doesn't work unless you share it with your people.* Otherwise they will think you are trying to manipulate them. That is particularly true with goal setting. Shared goal setting tends to get greater commitment from people and guarantees the setting of a realistic goal for the performance area."

"A realistic goal?" puzzled the veteran manager.

"A realistic goal is moderately difficult but achievable," explained Smith. "It's acceptable to you as a manager and it's possible for your people to accomplish. Let's go back to Jack. He has been setting up one appointment a day by phone. How many appointment calls are acceptable to you? How many are attainable by Jack?"

"How many does the best salesperson make?" inquired the veteran manager.

"Comparing Jack to the best won't encourage him. It will only discourage him," answered Smith. "Remember, we're using this method as a training tool, not as a punishment."

"What goal would you set?" asked the veteran, shrugging his shoulders.

"I'd probably say, 'Jack, let's see if you can make three appointment calls a day next week. How does that sound?'"

"So you have to be specific about the number and the time frame," commented the veteran.

"Exactly," said Smith. "What do you suppose would happen if I simply said to Jack, 'I'd like you to make more appointment calls. I don't think you have been making enough lately'?"

"He'd probably say OK," said the veteran, "and then not take it seriously."

"That's why I'd make a graph with Jack by my side," said Smith. "Then he'd know I was serious and know exactly what he had to do to get back into my good graces."

She removed another graph from the file she had gotten from her desk. "This was Jack's first goal-setting graph," said Smith as she handed the veteran the graph.

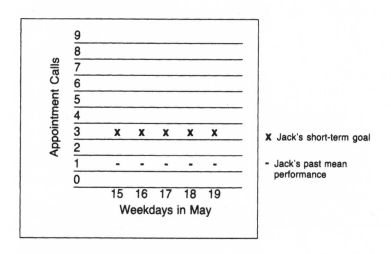

"You see, we plotted Jack's past mean performance (one call a day) and his short-term goal (three calls a day). That way he could see the difference between where he'd been and where he was headed," explained Smith.

"Why wouldn't you say you wanted Jack to make an appointment call for every sales visit he was going to make?" wondered the veteran.

"That might have been an appropriate goal in the long run," said Smith, "but in the short run you couldn't expect that kind of turnaround in behavior because Jack had obviously gotten himself into some bad work patterns. Just as you can't expect to lose twenty-five pounds today, but you do want some change. So we had to set a short-term goal with Jack, like three appointment calls a day."

"Short-term goal?" wondered the veteran.

"It's a first step," said Smith. "When you set up a performance-improvement program with people, remember not to set the end-result goal (in this case an appointment call for *every* sales visit—about six or seven calls per workday) as the goal that has to be reached before someone can feel a sense of accomplishment and deserve a praising; otherwise you might have to wait forever."

"I remember that concept now," said the veteran. "In the beginning, when working on performance, you need to set things up so you can catch people doing things approximately right (short-term goal), not exactly right (final goal)."

"Precisely," said Smith. "The journey to exactly right is make up of a whole series of approximately rights."

"So Rome can't be built in a day," said the veteran. "As a result, what you want to do is keep track of progress from present performance to the desired level. What's the best way to do that?"

"By involving people in coaching," said Smith. "As you know, once people are clear on what they are being asked to do, coaching is essentially observing their performance and giving them feedback on results. But the whole coaching process is set up by agreeing ahead of time with your people when and how you are going to give them feedback. That part of coaching is done during the Involve step."

"I would imagine," interrupted the veteran, "that by designing, with your people, the feedback system you are going to use, you are increasing the chances of their winning—accomplishing their goals."

"Exactly," said Smith. "Setting up a good feedback system through performance graphs is crucial if you hope to do any day-to-day coaching. That's why, with Jack, we agreed that for the first week I'd stop by his desk every day and review his phone log. I'd graph his performance and share it with him."

"What other coaching agreements did you make besides your daily visits?" asked the manager.

"Recording performance every day can be time-consuming," said Smith. "So we agreed to meet again after the first week to evaluate when Jack could begin to administer his own feedback."

"Administer his own feedback?" repeated the veteran.

"If I am having a performance problem with Jack, what I want to do is set up a graph that Jack is able to use. He can put his own check marks, stars, or whatever on the graph."

"Then he's able to say, 'Hey, I'm doing better,' or 'I'm doing worse,'" suggested the veteran manager. "He can even begin to praise or reprimand himself."

"Yes," said Smith. "Feedback that is self-administered can be immediate—as close to the performance as possible."

"At this point, what else did you involve Jack in?" asked the veteran.

"All I had left to do in the 'I' step in the PRICE system was to involve Jack in performance evaluation," said Smith.

"How did you intend to do that?" asked the veteran manager.

"When we set up the graph, Jack knew how his performance was going to be evaluated, but to complete his involvement in performance evaluation, we still had to decide what was in it for Jack if he improved," said Smith.

"What do you mean?" asked the veteran.

"What positive consequence will happen for Jack if he reaches his goal," Smith answered.

"Did I hear you say that you and Jack had to decide together? Didn't you just tell him?" responded the veteran.

what if it is money?

"If Jack had been less capable and committed, I would have determined the rewards. But Jack knew best what rewards would motivate him," explained Smith. "I asked Jack, 'What will motivate you to make more calls?' He said, 'If I make my quota, write me a note. I collect those things. I have every letter of commendation I've received since high school. But don't have your secretary type me some form letter. Write it by hand.'

"I thought that was a great idea. I said, 'What if you don't meet your quota?' He said, 'Come and tell me I deserve a reprimand. You probably won't even have to deliver it. But just knowing that you know I am slipping back to old behavior will get me back on track.'"

"Did you keep track of the praisings versus the number of reprimands?" laughed the veteran.

"It might sound funny," said Smith, "but I did exactly that. I started a log of praisings and reprimands. It worked beautifully. Now I keep a praising/reprimand log* on all my employees. It's just a list of names with *P*'s and *R*'s after each name with a shorthand note about what happened. It keeps me on track with One Minute Management."

---

*Ted Fletcher, manager, training and development, for the Nestlé Company, shared One Minute Management with one of his division managers, Ed Dippold. Now they are keeping praising and reprimand logs on each of their people in their New Jersey plant. Ed reports, "It really works! With union employees and foremen who rotate on shifts, it has kept communications clear and open."

"THAT makes sense," said the veteran manager. "So prior to actually coaching or evaluating performance, the consequences for goal accomplishment have to be agreed upon in the Involve (I) step of the PRICE system."

"In Jack's case," said Smith, "he knew what the goals (short- and long-term) were, how I was going to supervise or coach him, and how his performance would be evaluated, including the consequences he could expect for poor performance as well as for improved performance."

"Now that all those things were settled," interrupted the veteran, "Jack was ready to start improving his appointment-call behavior."

"Yes," said Smith. "And at that point, my role changed from involving Jack in decision making about establishing the necessary activators to observing his performance and managing the consequences."

"That's what coaching is all about," said the veteran. "Observing behavior and giving feedback on results—both praisings and reprimands. And that's when you began the 'C' or COACH step in PRICE."

"You've got it. Now I can show you how well Jack did," said Smith. "Here's his graph from the first week."

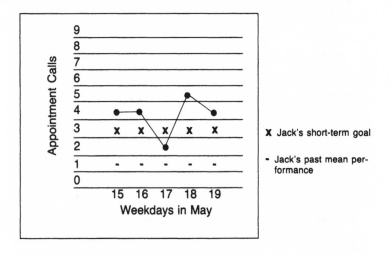

X Jack's short-term goal

- Jack's past mean performance

"That's great. He bettered his goal except on the third day," commented the veteran manager as he read the graph. "When did you tell him about his improvement, at your planned meeting at the end of the week?"

"Absolutely not," said Smith. "Remember a basic rule of feedback is that it should be immediate and specific. If the data flow is vague and delayed, it is not an effective training tool. And besides I had made an agreement with Jack that during the first week I'd stop by his desk daily, review his phone log, graph his performance, and share it with him."

"How specific would you be?" wondered the veteran manager.

"I'd actually use numbers," said Smith. "I'd say, 'You made your goal,' 'You bettered your goal by one,' or 'You missed your goal by one.' So once the goal is set, feedback relates specifically to the goal."

"OK. I see how the daily feedback with Jack went," said the veteran, "but how did you handle the meeting at the end of the week when you planned to evaluate whether Jack could begin to administer his own feedback or not?"

"I was happy with Jack's progress that first week," said Smith, "so I was willing to listen to any suggestions he might have about how I should monitor his performance and give him feedback. Remember, as people improve, you want to gradually turn over to them more and more of the responsibility for monitoring their own performance.

"Jack was very aware of his needs," observed Smith proudly. "He said, 'Look, if you leave me entirely alone, I'm going to feel abandoned. But I don't want you coming to my desk every day. It makes me nervous. For the next month let me do the daily graph myself and you come by on Fridays to check it out. If I need some help during the week, I'll come see you.'"

"So you worked out a new agreement with him," said the veteran. "Did you keep doing that until he performed like a winner in that part of his job?"

"Absolutely," said Smith. "I want to supervise my people closely only if they need it. As soon as they can perform on their own, I am ready to let go. In coaching you want to schedule fewer and fewer feedback meetings as people move gradually from their present level of performance to the desired level of performance. We have an expression that we use here that I think would be important for you to learn." She wrote on her pad:

*

*Achieving
Good Performance
Is
A Journey—
Not
A Destination*

*

"THAT'S well put," said the veteran. "Many managers just shout out destinations (goals) and then sit back and wait for people to reach them. What's helpful about the PRICE system is that it suggests that coaching is a process of managing the journey. I'm ready to move on to EVALUATE (E), the last step in the PRICE system. Are you?"

"Why not?" said Smith. "After all, evaluation and coaching go hand in hand. In fact, every time you give someone feedback you are evaluating. You want to continually determine how well performance is going in pinpointed areas. Are you getting the results you want? If not, why not?"

"If evaluation and coaching go hand in hand," said the veteran manager, "why do you have Evaluate as a separate step in the PRICE system?"

"Because most organizations have actual formal performance-review sessions," said Smith. "These sessions are held quarterly, semiannually, or only once a year. In the PRICE system we recommend that you graph and track performance in pinpointed One Minute goal areas for no longer than six weeks without having a formal evaluation session. Unless the person is a proven winner."

"What do you discuss in these sessions?" wondered the veteran.

"Nothing new," said Smith. "All we do is review what we have been talking about throughout the coaching progress. "It is a way to formally recognize progress and a time to evaluate future strategies. Can the manager turn over the supervision of the PRICE project(s) to the people involved or is direction and help still needed?"

"While evaluation in the PRICE system is a continuous process," said the veteran, "I don't get the feeling it is a punitive process. A One Minute Manager does not try to trip people up."

"David Berlo, one of the most thoughtful teachers and consultants I have ever met," said Smith, "gave me the best expression of that philosophy. He got interested in the training of whales. One day he asked some of his training friends in Florida whether they actually trained the whales by using some of the concepts we have been talking about in the coaching process. They said, 'Yes, with one addition.'"

"What was that?" wondered the veteran.

"Before they attempted to train the whales to do anything," said Smith, "the trainers told David, 'We feed them and make sure they're not hungry. And then we jump in the water and play with the whales until we have convinced them . . .'"

"Convinced them of what?" wondered the veteran manager.

"Let me write that down for you," said Smith, "because it underlies everything that One Minute Management stands for." She reached over and borrowed the veteran manager's note pad and began to write.

*

We
Mean
Them
No
Harm

*

"That's a powerful statement," said the veteran manager as he read what Alice Smith had written. "That's all about trust, isn't it?"

"It sure is," said Smith. "David is writing a book entitled *I Mean You No Harm* because he feels that most of the performance review and evaluation systems that companies set up in our country suggest the very opposite."

"Now that you mention it," said the veteran, "that is so true. Most evaluation systems suggest that there always have to be winners and losers."

"That's just not part of the philosophy of the One Minute Manager," said Smith.

"So, when you talk about evaluation in the PRICE system," said the veteran, "you are always trying to find out whether you are getting the desired results. If you are, your people get recognized and praised. And if you're not, they get redirected or reprimanded depending on whether the problem is one of ability or motivation. Are there any other reasons why you wouldn't be getting the desired results?"

"Performance can break down at every step of the PRICE system," responded Smith. "You might have pinpointed an irrelevant area. Or you might be recording data ineffectively. In involving your people you might have agreed upon too low or too high a goal, your feedback might be erratic, or your consequences not sufficiently motivating."

"So you are taking some significant responsibility for ensuring that your people perform well," said the veteran manager.

"Most definitely," said Smith. "My job as a manager is not just to sit back, cross my arms, look stern, and evaluate. It's to roll up my sleeves and be responsive to people and what they need to perform well."

"So you have to keep your eyes and ears open," interjected the veteran. "I would imagine you often go back to Pinpoint and start the process again. So PRICE is a continuous process."

"Exactly," said Smith. "That's why we like to show PRICE almost like a dial on the telephone." She pointed to a plaque on the wall. It read:

Putting the One Minute Manager to Work

A Summary of
the
PRICE SYSTEM

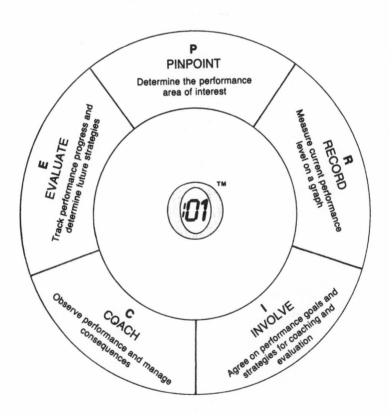

"**T**HAT'S great. Now I can dial *P* for *performance*," said the veteran with a smile.

"Let me emphasize one last thing about PRICE," said Smith. "You can use it to achieve excellence in all parts of your life. Set up a PRICE system for losing weight or running. Set one up for your kids' chores or school grades. If you involve your family you can make a New Year's resolution become a reality rather than another unfulfilled promise to yourself and others."

"It gives me another way to take what I know about One Minute Management and really put it to work in an organized fashion," said the veteran manager.

"It certainly has been key to our performance," said Smith.

"Have you ever had anyone resist paying the PRICE?" asked the veteran manager.

"Why don't you ask the One Minute Manager about Hank?" smiled Smith as she got up and led the veteran to the door.

"Yes, I guess I have taken enough of your time," said the veteran manager. "I've found this very practical and I appreciate your willingness to share your secrets with me."

"They're only secrets," responded Smith, "because people act as though they never knew them. Actually they're just common sense put to use."

As the veteran walked back to the One Minute Manager's office, he was amazed at how true that phrase was—common sense put to use.

When he got to the One Minute Manager's office, the veteran was greeted with a warm smile. "The PRICE is right, isn't it?" the One Minute Manager laughed.

"It sure is," said the veteran manager. "It really makes sense, but I have one question. Who is Hank?"

The One Minute Manager began to laugh. "I thought it was only a matter of time before someone told you about Hank. Why don't you sit down," said the One Minute Manager, "so I can tell you about him.

"When I first came here I heard about Hank from Steve Mulvany, a productivity-improvement consultant who had worked with our company. Steve said, 'Watch out for Hank when you start training the foremen about One Minute Management. He's one tough guy.' I got the impression that converting Hank to One Minute Management would be like persuading a charging rhino to rethink his strategy.

"The stories about Hank were widespread. He was almost a legend in his own time. For instance, I was told that one morning he got so mad at one of his people that he literally (I checked it out later with Hank and it was true) picked him up and hung him by his overalls on a nail and left him there until lunch."

"Now, how could anybody do that?" asked the veteran manager.

"Hank is about five feet nine by five feet nine and strong," said the One Minute Manager. "When he sits at the end of our thirty-inch-wide conference table he is about as wide as the table. He has arms as big as my thighs. His head sits on his shoulders as if he literally had no neck."

"He doesn't sound like a real attractive human being," said the veteran.

"No, he's not or at least he wasn't," said the One Minute Manager. "His eyes were bloodshot, he had an old grumpy voice, and he walked like a bear on the prowl.

"I first met Hank," continued the One Minute Manager, "at a training session. When I came here and began to implement One Minute Management, I initially did most of the training myself. I arrived early to the session where I met Hank. While I was setting up training materials in the front of the conference room, I suddenly got the feeling somebody was watching me. I turned around and there was Hank sitting alone at the other end of the conference room."

"How did you know it was him?" asked the veteran manager.

"I just knew," said the One Minute Manager. "Especially when I got no response to a smile. I could just feel his eyes looking through me."

"What did you say?" interrupted the veteran. "I feel as if I'm in the middle of another soap opera."

"Nothing then," said the One Minute Manager, "but I knew he was watching my every move. At least I sensed he was. When I started my session he sat quietly until I said, 'One of the keys to motivating your people is to catch them doing something right. When that occurs,' I asked, 'what should you do as a manager?' Everyone said reward or praise them, except Hank."

"How did you know he didn't agree?" said the veteran manager.

"Hank raised his hand," said the One Minute Manager, "and I thought to myself, 'Well, the session is over. Pack your bags.' He said, 'I want to say something,' and I said, 'Sure!'

"Hank said, 'I just want you to know that I use punishment and it works.'

"I looked at him and thought to myself, 'I'll bet it does.' What are you going to say to someone like Hank? He could have said that the sky was green and I would have agreed right there that the sky was green.

"When I got my composure, I said, 'That's interesting, Hank. Would you be willing to share the pros of punishment with the group?'

"He said, 'Sure! There are three: It's easy. It's fast. And it makes me feel good.'

"Looking at his size, I said to myself, 'I'll bet it works for you.' Then I said, 'If those are the pros, Hank, are there any cons to using too much punishment?'

"Hank smiled and said, 'I can't think of one.'

"I said, 'I can think of three areas too much punishment can affect—efficiency rates, absenteeism, and turnover.'

"Hank stared at me because he knew what I was thinking. He had the lowest efficiency rates in the plant. Now he knew that but I had heard his excuses: 'I have the toughest department' and 'I'm on a swing shift and everyone knows that swing shifts traditionally have the lowest productivity.'

"Absenteeism—Hank consistently had twenty percent of his people absent so he had eight out of ten at work most days. The personnel folks joked that without Hank's department they would have to lay off one staff member. They were busy every day processing transfer requests, terminations, or hiring for his department.

"Turnover—his was the highest in the plant. But I had heard him say, 'I manage the worst department there is and everyone likes to transfer out.'

"When it was obvious I was baiting him, Hank said, 'OK, boss. What do you expect me to do differently with bums like I've got? They live to pay for their booze. And besides, I don't like them and they don't like me.'

"I said, 'Hank, I know you probably think these sessions are a waste of time. But will you give me a chance?'

"'OK!' Hank said. 'But I'm not counting on anything.'

"After I had talked about the need to start any performance-improvement program with pinpointing the problem and then recording present performance, I shared the importance of the daily printout from the computer for tracking progress and giving people feedback. You see, in our operation the foremen get good information on performance."

"As you were speaking, what was Hank doing?" asked the veteran manager.

"He just sat there with his arms crossed," said the One Minute Manager. "There was no expression on his face."

"After the meeting, much to my surprise, Hank came up to me and said, 'Look, I think this stuff is probably useless. But I'd like to increase my efficiency rate. Any smart ideas?'

"'Every day you get a printout from the computer on the efficiency of each of your machines for the day before,' I replied. 'Since you have a one man per machine operation, this information tells you how each of your guys is doing. All I want you to do is make a graph for everyone and at the beginning of every morning, fill in the efficiency ratings on the graphs and then walk around and show each guy what his efficiency was from the day before. That's all I want you to do.'

"'OK,' said Hank. 'I'll give it a try even though I don't think it will work.'

"The next morning, I went down to see what happened," continued the One Minute Manager. "Hank got the printout from the computer and transferred the information to graphs for each of his people and then walked over to his first guy and said, 'Listen, don't give me any crap about the number on here. Just look at it.' And then he showed the guy his efficiency rating.

"I thought to myself, 'This is going to be a disaster,' so I said to Hank, 'Just show them the number and don't say anything else. Just say, "You got eighty-six percent efficiency yesterday." "You got ninety-four." "You got seventy-five."'

"When he said to the next guy, 'You got eighty-three percent efficiency yesterday,' the guy said, 'Hank, get out of here and get away from me. We're going to call the union. Knock this stuff off. Leave us alone. You've left us alone for years unless we did something wrong, so just get out of here.'

"Hank said to me, 'I told you they don't like me.'

"I said, 'Hank, keep trying.'

"Hank kept showing his guys their efficiency rates even though they were giving him a hard time and not even looking at their graphs. Then after about four days I could see them starting to look when he came along showing them their scores. They were starting to look at the graphs because they were beginning to get feedback and were able to compare how they did yesterday to the day before, and the day before that."

"And the comparisons were against themselves, not the other guys," interrupted the veteran.

"Yes," said the One Minute Manager. "We find it more constructive to have people competing against themselves and a performance standard rather than competing with each other."

"What happened next?" interrupted the veteran manager, anxious to get back to hearing about Hank.

"Hank told his people, 'Listen, you guys, I'm getting sick and tired of giving this feedback to you all. From now on, anybody with eighty-five percent or higher efficiency, I'll come and show you your rating. But if you didn't get eighty-five percent, you don't deserve to talk to me.'"

"Let's see if I can fit this story into the PRICE system," suggested the veteran. "When Hank said he wanted to improve efficiency he was pinpointing the problem. That's 'P.' When he made the graphs from the computer printout he was into 'R' for record. And when he began showing his folks their efficiency ratings in the beginning he was involving them, even if he was a little autocratic. That's 'I.' Now by deciding to talk only with people with eighty-five percent or higher efficiency, it sounds as if Hank was beginning to manage consequences and to coach. That's 'C.' That decision was made at his own kind of evaluation session: 'E.'"

"Exactly!" said the One Minute Manager. "You really learned the PRICE system quickly!"

"I just love the simplicity of it all," said the veteran manager.

"It was funny to see Hank," continued the One Minute Manager, "walk up to a guy and then, reading that his efficiency rate was below eighty-five, walk right by him without showing him his graph or saying a word. The expression on that person's face was priceless. He acted as if Hank had stabbed him in the back."

"I bet pretty soon everyone was getting over eighty-five percent efficiency," said the veteran manager.

"You better believe it," said the One Minute Manager. "After a week or so Hank called them all back together. He said, 'Ninety-five percent efficiency or I don't come to your machine.' It was amazing how their efficiency scores climbed."

"That's amazing, considering that all Hank was doing was giving them the information," said the veteran.

"Right," said the One Minute Manager. "He didn't say they did well; he didn't say they did badly. Just the fact that Hank would show up at their machines was important to them.

"He did this," continued the One Minute Manager, "for some time. Then, after about a month he gave each of them his own graph and stopped coming to their machines but he would leave the printout from the computer on his desk. I swear to you, nine out of ten guys would run over there on their break time to see what they got and go back and fill in their graphs.

"Then he started to circle in red the guys who got ninety-five percent. Can you believe it? A bunch of hard-nosed guys like this talking about whether they got a red circle that day. They thought it was really something special if they got a red circle."

"What was happening to the performance in Hank's department all this time?" asked the veteran manager.

"It was going up like a spaceship on the graph," said the One Minute Manager. "At the same time his absenteeism and tardiness were going down too. The other foremen didn't believe it. They thought Hank was cheating on the data. I knew he wasn't because I was watching the data all the time."

"What did he do next?" asked the veteran manager.

"One day," said the One Minute Manager, "he brought all his guys together and said, 'You guys have really been increasing your efficiency. I'll tell you what I'll do. My wife makes the finest pumpkin bread you've ever tasted, so if every guy in this department gets one hundred percent, I'll have her bring in pumpkin bread at lunchtime tomorrow for everyone.'

"I wasn't at the meeting but I heard about it from the grapevine. I went to see him. I said, 'Hank, pumpkin bread as a motivator? It's not going to work.'

"He said, 'That's what you think. Let me do it.'

"I said, 'Hank, you can do anything you want'— as if I could stop him."

"Hank didn't even walk around and watch them," continued the One Minute Manager. "They monitored themselves. For example, if someone left his machine to get something or do something, one of the guys would yell, 'Hey, where are you going? You get back to work.'"

"Did everyone get one hundred percent efficiency?" asked the veteran manager.

"You better believe it," said the One Minute Manager. "No exceptions. So at lunchtime the next day Hank's wife brought in these platters of pumpkin bread. You never saw anything go so fast in your life. They loved it.

"I thought that was something, so I tried to replicate what Hank did for all of the departments.

"I called in my key people and told them I would be willing to buy lunch the next day for every department that got one hundred percent in efficiency on any given day."

"What did your people think?" asked the veteran.

"Everyone thought it was a great idea," said the One Minute Manager. "We had these little coupons printed up that the employees could use on the 'roach coach.'"

"The roach coach?" wondered the veteran.

"That's an affectionate name for the food truck that goes around to plants, selling all kinds of goodies," said the One Minute Manager. "Our folks often wait to eat lunch until it stops here.

"While I thought my plan was a good idea, it went over like a lead balloon. In fact, people got hostile. They were saying things like: 'This is ridiculous!' 'Don't have us do five hundred dollars more productivity in exchange for a two dollar food coupon. We're insulted.'"

"What happened?" asked the veteran manager.

"I was confused," said the One Minute Manager, "so I asked Hank to come see me."

"So Hank's now a consultant to top management," laughed the veteran.

"It took courage to admit I needed advice from Hank," confessed the One Minute Manager.

"What did Hank think of the program?" wondered the veteran manager.

"He had elected not to do the coupon program," said the One Minute Manager. "In fact, he was one of the leaders of the revolt. That's why I wanted to talk to him—to find out why he wouldn't participate in the coupon program.

"When Hank arrived at my office, I asked him, 'Why aren't you involved in the coupon program?'

"Hank leaned over to me and put his finger right in my face and said, 'You tried to bribe the employees. You offered them two dollars on the roach coach to increase productivity. Let me tell you how I and the other men felt about that. We were damn mad. We felt used and insulted.'

"Then he took his finger away from my face, paused, and stared in my eyes for what seemed like an endless moment. 'Let me tell you one other thing,' Hank said as he broke the silence. 'You're good. You've done a tremendous job putting the One Minute Manager to work here. We think you're better than that kind of bribery stuff.'

"Then Hank smiled and said, 'How's that for a One Minute Reprimand?'

"I'll have to admit that being on the end of a reprimand from Hank wasn't the most comfortable experience I've ever had," said the One Minute Manager.

"After I got my composure back, I said, 'I realize my mistake, but how was what I did different from your pumpkin bread?'

"'My wife made that pumpkin bread,' said Hank. 'I put myself out and so did she. You offered to give us two dollars to use on the roach coach. That's an insult and a bribe.'

"'So my lunch coupon,' I said, 'was insulting because it wasn't personal and it didn't involve any emotional commitment from me?'

"'Right,' said Hank. 'You have done a fantastic job around here introducing your concepts of One Minute Management and teaching us the ABC's. Most of us are willing to pay the PRICE to get good performance. The people you have working for you are winners and you shouldn't take the ball away from them. Don't try to sprinkle motivation from on high.'

"'I understand what you are saying, Hank,' I replied, 'and I appreciate your honesty.'

"That's OK,' said Hank. 'I've learned a lot here and there's no reason why I can't help you learn, too.'

"We both smiled and shook hands."

"Hank's quite a guy, isn't he?"* said the veteran manager.

"He certainly is," said the One Minute Manager. "It's people like him who have really made our efforts worthwhile here."

"And he's taught me to put the things I've learned here into a human perspective," added the veteran. "Speaking of the things I've learned, I'd like to sum it all up for you. I want to be certain I've got it all straight."

"Go right ahead," said the One Minute Manager.

---

*The Hank story is based on a real character. He models characteristics of many of the outstanding supervisors we have worked with over the years. Steve Mulvany, president of Management Tools, Inc., in Orange, California, originally developed the story while Bob Lorber was president and Steve was senior vice-president of PSI, a productivity-improvement company that conducted a project in Hank's plant. Steve supervised this project and since then has immortalized Hank as "Sid" in his seminars and presentations around the world.

"**F**IRST, I cleared up some questions I had about the three secrets of One Minute Management: One Minute Goal Setting, One Minute Praisings, and One Minute Reprimands," remembered the veteran manager. "Second, I've learned that the ABC's of Management (the Activators, the resulting Behavior, and the appropriate Consequences) help sequence those secrets in a way that makes them usable. And third, the PRICE System gives me a good handle on how to put the One Minute Manager to work in a systematic way that can be shared with everyone. It turns the secrets into skills and moves the application of One Minute Management beyond individuals to work groups and the organization as a whole."

The One Minute Manager smiled at he listened to the veteran. He loved to see the excitement that learning new things sparked in people.

"Sounds as if you have everything pretty straight," commented the One Minute Manager.

"I think I've got it," said the veteran. "I can't thank you enough for sharing with me what you know and have learned about management."

"It's my pleasure," said the One Minute Manager. "All that knowledge is to be shared. Let me leave you with one last thought. The best way to learn to be a One Minute Manager and to use what you have learned is to start to do it. The important thing is not that you do it right, but that you get under way. We have a saying here:

*

*Anything
Worth Doing
Does Not
Have To Be Done
Perfectly—
At First*

*

"THAT'S so true," said the veteran. "I'm really committed to getting started."

"It's not your commitment that I'm worried about," said the One Minute Manager. "It's your commitment to your commitment. For example, people say diets don't work. Diets work just fine— it's people who don't work. They break their commitment to their commitment to lose weight. I don't want you to do that with putting the One Minute Manager to work."

"What you're saying makes sense of what a friend of mine told me," said the veteran. "He told me I should give up trying. I should either do it or not do it."

"That's just what I was getting at," said the One Minute Manager. "To illustrate it, would you try to pick up that pen on the desk?"

The veteran went over to the desk and picked up the pen.

"I told you to try to pick up the pen. I didn't tell you to pick it up," said the One Minute Manager.

The veteran smiled.

"You got it," said the One Minute Manager. "You're either going to do it or not going to do it. Saying 'I'll try' just sets up all your past patterns which will result in your not doing it."

"Thanks for that final advice," said the veteran. "I certainly don't want to be the guy hanging on to the branch on the side of the mountain, yelling, 'Is there anybody else up there?'"

With that said, the veteran got up and put his hand out to the One Minute Manager. "I'm going to do it," he said with sincerity.

WHEN the veteran manager left the One Minute Manager's office, he was excited about implementing what he had learned. He was committed to his commitment.

The next day he began to do just that. He did not wait until he could do everything he had learned exactly right. He knew if he waited he would never get started, so he shared what he had learned with all his people, and they in turn shared it with their people. Everyone supported each other's efforts to put One Minute Management to work.

As he worked with his people, the veteran manager learned that four systems needed to be set up in the organization to make One Minute Management pay off. Employees needed to know: what they were being asked to do (accountability system); what good behavior looked like (performance-data system); how well they were doing (feedback system); and what they would get for good performance (recognition system).

Pretty soon, everyone in the veteran's organization set up PRICE projects for each One Minute Goal. The goals themselves identified the *pinpointed* areas of interest. Present performance on each of these goals was *recorded*. Then each employee was *involved* in goal setting, as well as in establishing coaching and counseling strategies. Then *coaching* began. Managers were responsive to their people's needs for supervision. Everybody wanted the others to win. When *evaluation* came around, progress was reviewed and new goals set.

Pretty soon the inevitable happened:

THE VETERAN MANAGER WAS SUCCESSFUL IN
PUTTING THE ONE MINUTE MANAGER TO WORK
AND IT MADE A DIFFERENCE —

People not only felt better, they performed better. And more important, putting the One Minute Manager to work made a difference where it really counted—on the bottom line. Production increased, quality improved, sales skyrocketed, and retention and attendance of employees surpassed all the companies in the area.

Everywhere the veteran manager went he shared what he had learned with others. One Minute Management soon became known as **Theory W.** The One Minute Manager said, "You can have your Theory X, Theory Y, and Theory Z. We call One Minute Management **Theory W** because it works."

Wherever the veteran manager went, he always told people who had learned how to put the One Minute Manager to work . . .

*

*Keep Your
Commitment
To
Your Commitment*

*And
Share
It
With
Others*

*

:01™ *Concept Praisings*

We would like to give a public praising to the following people whose conceptual contributions were invaluable to us in preparing this book:

David Berlo for his thoughtful analysis of why organizations are not good places for people to be.

Tom Connellan, *Aubrey Daniels*, and *Larry Miller* for teaching us many things about productivity improvement.

Werner Erhard for what he taught us about making life work and keeping your commitments.

Paul Hersey for his creativity and ability to integrate applied behavioral science theory.

Spencer Johnson for attaching the One Minute concept to praisings and reprimands.

Fred Luthans and *Robert Kreitner* for one of the first conceptualizations of the ABC's.

David McClelland for his pioneer work on achievement motivation.

Gerald Nelson for developing the One Minute Scolding, the forerunner of the One Minute Reprimand.

George Odiorne for his work on goal setting (MBO) and the "activity trap."

B. F. Skinner for his classic work on reinforcement theory.

Rick Tate for coining the phrase "Feedback Is the Breakfast of Champions."

⑴™ *Personal Praisings*

We would like to give a public praising to a number of the important people in our lives who have influenced and supported us.

Ken Blanchard would like to praise:

Spencer Johnson, my co-author of *The One Minute Manager*, for being my writing partner, publishing mentor, and friend.

Kelsey Tyson for his creative marketing of the original version of *The One Minute Manager* and for his untiring dedication and devoted friendship.

Margaret McBride for being my literary agent, friend and mediator, and constant support.

All the folks at William Morrow and Company, Inc., particularly *Pat Golbitz* and *Larry Hughes*, for believing in Spencer and me and *The One Minute Manager*, and *Al Marchioni* and his people for distributing and selling the book.

The following top managers who believed in me and *The One Minute Manager* and gave us the kind of support that helped make the dream of a best-selling book a reality:

Roy Anderson	Dave Hanna	Bud Robinson
Rhett Butler	David Jones	Mike Rose
Jim DeLapa	Lou Neeb	Don Smith
Bob Davis	Ernie Renaud	Jere Thompson

Michael and *Nina Shandler*, two very talented writers and trainers, who literally lived with the manuscript during the middle drafts, and working with me, helped this book begin to change from a good book to what I think is a "super" book.

Ken Haff, Laurie Hawkins, Drea Zigarmi, and *Pat Zigarmi*, my colleagues and friends, for their ever-present love, support, and helpful feedback.

Paul Hersey for being my mentor, friend, father and brother—all wrapped up in one.

Eleanor Terndrup for being my talented secretary and second mother. From start to finish of this manuscript Eleanor was always there way beyond the call of duty.

Bernadette McDonald for her unfailing devotion and commitment to quality work. Without her typing and clerical skills during the middle drafts, this book would never have become a reality.

Lynette Grage for worrying about where we were going to get the money to pay for all my dreams.

Regina Rule, Pat Nekervis, and *Donna Hagen* for their constant hard work and caring about *The One Minute Manager*.

A special thanks to my mother and father, *Dorothy and Ted Blanchard*. Mom has been a constant inspiration and joy all my life but especially since Dad's passing. While he has not been here to share this One Minute Manager phenomenon with me, I have felt his support.

Bob Lorber would like to praise:

Gordon Anderson for giving me the opportunity to form my new Productivity Implementation Company and for teaching me that the United States is only one part of the world.

Linda Belton for her loyalty and extraordinary competence as my assistant during many of the productivity-implementation years.

Gene Bryan for making the computer come alive and computer-aided management a reality. And for being my co-author in our new book *The Profit Gap.*

Fred Chaney for being a mentor and for giving me the opportunity to found and build Performance Systems Improvement (PSI).

Bob Elliott for taking a risk, believing in me, and letting me personally implement our first productivity-improvement program.

Ethan Jackson for his exceptional business and personal advice and unconditional friendship. For modeling the critical balance of family and business and opening my eyes to the spiritual side of life.

Kef Kamai for being my partner, friend, and compadre and for making me pay attention to my health and physical fitness. For being Tracie's godfather and always being there when I need him.

Larry Miller for being an invaluable colleague and friend. And for being my East Coast partner in our productivity-improvement business.

Jim Morrell for his guidance, friendship, and influence on my career path.

Pat Murray for being my partner in planning, top-management team building, and crisis resolution and for teaching me the full meaning of integrity.

Bud Ogden for opening the world of the coal industry and all its beauty, hardships, and real people, and for the major opportunities he personally provided.

Mark Rosen for being my first colleague in productivity implementation and for the many years of being a brother and friend.

Carl Samuels for his unselfish love, advice, and openness.

Donna Sillman for helping Ken and me edit the first draft of our book, and for staying in California to support the formation of our new company.

Fran Tarkenton for his energy, inspiration, and contributions to the field of productivity improvement.

Ed Winguth for always believing in me and in his continued help on complex career decisions.

A special thank you to my mother and father, *Rose and Jules Lorber*. They always understand me, support me, express their love, and practice the principles we have written about in our book.

About the Authors

Few people have made a more positive and lasting impact on the day-to-day management of people and companies than **Ken Blanchard**. He is the author of several bestselling books, including the blockbuster international bestseller *The One Minute Manager* and the giant business bestsellers *Leadership and the One Minute Manager, Raving Fans*, and *Gung Ho!* His books have combined sales of more than eighteen million copies in more than twenty-five languages. Ken is the chief spiritual officer of The Ken Blanchard Companies, a worldwide human resource development company. He is also cofounder of the Lead Like Jesus Ministries, a nonprofit organization dedicated to inspiring and equipping people to be servant leaders in the marketplace. Ken and his wife, Margie, live in San Diego and work with their son Scott, daughter Debbie, and Debbie's husband, Humberto Medina.

Dr. Robert L. Lorber is president of The Lorber Kamai Consulting Group, a firm formed in 1976. The organization has implemented productivity improvement systems for companies on five continents and its client roster includes Kraft Foods, Gillette, American Express, Mattel, Wells Fargo, Pillsbury, Pfizer, and many other midsize and Fortune 500 companies.

Dr. Lorber is an internationally recognized expert and published author on executive coaching, performance management, leadership, teamwork, culture, and developing strategy. He is one of the leading resources worldwide on executive coaching with chief executive officers and company presidents. As a professional speaker, Dr. Lorber has delivered presentations for profit and nonprofit audiences throughout the world. He is also the coauthor, with Riaz Khadem, of *One Page Management*.

Dr. Lorber works with numerous boards of directors on governance and effective board participation. Currently he serves as chairman of the Dean's Advisory Council for the Graduate School of Management at the University of California at Davis, the UC Davis School of Medicine's Board of Visitors, and many other corporate and not-for-profit boards.

Dr. Lorber is an associate professor at his alma mater—the Graduate School of Management at UC Davis—where he teaches courses on leadership. Dr. Lorber received a master's degree in sociology and a doctorate in organizational psychology. He lives in Davis, California, with his wife, Sandy, and their three daughters, Tracie, Lindie, and Kaylie.

Services Available

The Ken Blanchard Companies®—a global leader in workplace learning, productivity, performance, and leadership effectiveness—offers situational leadership programs that show people how to excel as self-leaders and as leaders of others. Many Blanchard® programs for teams, customer loyalty, change management, and leadership effectiveness blend the use of assessments with instructor-led and online learning. Blanchard® continually researches and shares best practices for improving performance in the workplace, while its world-class trainers and coaches drive sustainability of these approaches into all levels of organizations and help people make the shift from learning to doing. To learn more, visit www.kenblanchard.com, or contact us at +1.800.728.6000 from the U.S., or +1.760.489.5005 from anywhere.

Lorber Kamai Consulting is a firm specializing in productivity and performance improvement. It also focuses on CEO and senior executive team coaching, executive team development, and strategic planning implementation. Robert Lorber also consults with large family businesses regarding succession and transition. For more information visit www.lorberkamai.com, contact rllorber@ucdavis.edu, or contact by phone at +1.530.758.6443.